Book 1

Edition 3.0 – Oct 2022

Answer key updated papers 2 and 4

Disclaimer

BGS Books and this publication have no association with the Consortium of Selective Schools in Essex (CSSE), or any other schools or examination boards.

Every effort has been made to ensure that the information contained in this book is accurate; however, we are not responsible for anyone failing any part of their exam as a result of the information contained in this book or on our website www.bgsbooks.com

British Grammar School Books

About this Book

Our papers have been written with the intention of providing quality exam question practice at the same standard and level of difficulty as the current CSSE 11+ exams.

After each paper is completed, record the score achieved for each question in the 'Topic Scorecard Matrix' at the back of this book.

To keep papers realistic, not every topic is covered in every paper, so all papers should be completed before identifying those topics with the lowest percentage score.

Twenty-Two topics have appeared in the CSSE papers from 2015 onwards, all of which are covered in this book.

Refer to the scorecard at the end of the book for the question numbers mapped to each topic.

1. Use four rules / BODMAS – both basic and worded problems
2. Fraction questions and their equivalents
3. Basic Algebra and Nth rule problem solving
4. Angles on a straight line or triangle, identify angle types
5. Read and plot Co-ordinates and perform transformations
6. Mean (Average), Median and Range
7. Square, Cube and Prime numbers (less than 100)
8. Tables and Data Interpretation
9. Number Problems (Number machines, Missing Numbers)
10. Ordering and Rounding Numbers
11. Calculating Percentages
12. Nets and Shapes
13. Probability
14. Reading Scales
15. Converting Units
16. Basic Speed, Distance or Time type questions
17. Calculate Area, Perimeter, Volume
18. Interpret different chart types, including Bar, Pie, Venn
19. Ratio and Proportion, Factors and Multiples
20. Time and calculate time intervals
21. Money Problems
22. Length, Distance, Mass, and Weight

B|G|S
British Grammar School Books

11+ CSSE Mock

Mathematics Paper 1

60 Minutes

The questions in this paper are worth 60 marks

Attempt all the questions, writing your answers clearly

If you cannot answer a question, leave it and go on to the next one

Use any time you have left to check your answers and go back to any unanswered questions

The numbers in brackets are the marks available for each question

Do NOT use a calculator

PAGE	SCORE	
	Marks	Total
2		8
3		6
4		5
5		6
6		5
7		3
8		3
9		4
10		4
11		7
12		4
13		5
TOTAL:		60

Question	ANSWER	MARKS R	T
1 (a) What number is half way between 5.9 and 6.3?			(1)
(b) What number is half way between -5 and 15?			(1)
2 Fill in the missing numbers in the sequences below:			
(a) 13 , 22 , 31 , 40 , ___ , 58			(1)
(b) 5 , 5.75 , ___ , 7.25 , 8 , 8.75			(1)
(c) 65 , 54.5 , 44 , 33.5 , 23 , ___			(1)
3 (a) A bucket weighs 3kg when filled with sand. If the bucket weighs 300g when empty, work out the weight of the sand in grams.	g		(1)
(b) Sandra has two cats, Molly and Smudge. Molly weighs 5.75kg. Smudge is 120 grams lighter. How much does Smudge weigh?	Kg		(1)
(c) The weight of five 2p coins is 7g. Find the weight of £6 worth of 2p coins.	Kg		(1)

SCORE 8

Question	ANSWER	MARKS R	T

4 The diagram shows how to convert temperature from °F to °C.

°F ➡ [- 32] [x 5] [÷] ➡ °C

(a) If a temperature of 95 °F converts into 35 °C, what is the missing number in the division box shown?

(1)

(b) Water boils at 100 °C. What is the temperature in °F?

(1)

5 Andrea draws four identical triangles to form a square.

(a) Using the information provided, write down the coordinates of triangle points A, B and C.

(12, 0)

(-4, -4)

A (__ , __)

B (__ , __)   (3)

C (__ , __)

(b) If the coordinate B is reflected in the Y-axis, what would the new coordinates be?

(__ , __)   (1)

SCORE 6

3

Question	ANSWER	MARKS R	T

6 The table below shows how the total number of Coronavirus cases increased over the first 3 months of 2021 in the UK.

COUNTRY	JAN	FEB	MAR
England	2,322,000	3,432,000	3,696,000
Northern Ireland	81,000	117,000	126,000
Scotland	135,000	156,000	168,000
Wales	162,000	195,000	210,000
UK Total	**2,700,000**	**3,900,000**	**4,200,000**

(a) Calculate the percentage increase in UK infections from Jan to Feb. Answer to 2 decimal places.

(1)

(b) In Feb, what percentage of the UK infections were in England?

(1)

(c) By Feb, 6% of the UK population had caught coronavirus. What is the size of the UK population in millions?

(1)

(d) The percentage increase from Dec to Jan in Wales was 8%. Calculate how many people were infected in Wales in Dec 2020?

(1)

(e) By March, 7 out of 8 infected people did not have any Covid symptoms. How many people in the UK did have symptoms?

(1)

SCORE

5

4

Question	ANSWER	MARKS R | T

7 Three squirrels collect a pile of 40 nuts to eat for dinner.
The first squirrel eats one quarter of the nuts.
The second squirrel then eats a fifth of the remaining nuts.
The third squirrel then finishes half of what is left.

(a) How many nuts did the first squirrel eat? (1)

(b) How many nuts were left over after the second squirrel ate? (1)

(c) How many nuts were left over after all three squirrels had eaten? (1)

8 (a) One of the angles in a right-angled triangle is 46 degrees. What is the angle of the other acute angle? (1)

(b) One of the angles in a triangle is 60°. One of the remaining two angles is three times larger than the other angle. What is the largest angle in the triangle? (1)

(c) If the time on a clock is midnight and I turn the large hand 150° degrees clockwise, what time will it be? (1)

SCORE 6

5

Question	ANSWER	MARKS R	T

9 The table below shows the ticket prices at the local cinema.

Cinema Tickets	Morning Showing	Afternoon Showing
Adult	£7.99	£10.00
Child	£4.99	£6.99
Student	£3.25	£3.25
Upgrades: 3D Screenings £1.50 extra per ticket		

(a) Brenda buys two child tickets and twice as many student tickets to watch a 3D movie in the morning. What is the total cost?

(1)

(b) How much does Brenda save in total by buying all the tickets for the morning show instead of the afternoon?

(1)

(c) If Adam spends £47.94 on adult tickets, how many did he buy?

(1)

10 The temperatures from Monday to Saturday are shown below in degrees Celsius.

Mon	Tues	Weds	Thurs	Fri	Sat
26	17	20	22	23	18

(a) What is the average temperature from Monday to Saturday?

(1)

(b) The average temperature increases by 1°C when including Sunday. What was the temperature on Sunday?

(1)

SCORE

5

Question	ANSWER	MARKS	
		R	T

11 Shown below is a net to make a cube. Three of its sides have different patterns.

On each net below, mark an X in the correct box so that it matches that shown above.

(a)

(1)

(b)

(1)

(c)

(1)

SCORE	
	3

Question	ANSWER	MARKS	
		R	T

12 In each of the following questions, write down the weight in KG of each object.

(a)

(1)

(b)

(1)

(c)

(1)

SCORE

3

Question	ANSWER	MARKS	
		R	T

13 Eugene lives in England where distances on road signs are displayed in miles.
She wants to travel to Paris, where signs are displayed in Kilometres.
1 mile = 1.6 km

(a) Eugene drives 70 miles from London to Dover.
How many kilometres has she travelled?

(1)

(b) From Dover Eugene catches a ferry to Calais which is 31 miles away. From Calais she then drives 291km to Paris.
How many km has she travelled in total from Dover to Paris?

(1)

(c) Eugene returns home using the same route.
How many miles will she have travelled in total?

(1)

14 In 1742, a famous Mathematician called Christian Goldbach claimed that:

> Every **even** number greater than two is the sum of **two prime** numbers.

How many pairs of prime numbers can sum to 36?

(1)

SCORE

4

9

Question	ANSWER	MARKS R	T

15 Bob buys a carton of orange juice for himself.

The carton is in the shape of a cuboid.

Its height is 9cm, width 6cm and depth 3cm as shown in the picture.

The carton is full with juice.

9cm

3cm

6cm

(a) Work out surface area of the carton.

(1)

(b) When the carton is full, what volume of juice does it hold?

(1)

(c) If Bob drinks a third, what volume of juice is remaining?

(1)

(d) If Bob buys 8 cartons of juice, how many 1 litre jugs can he fill completely?

(1)

SCORE

4

Question	ANSWER	MARKS
		R	T

16 Fifty adults were asked if they had ever visited France or Spain.

22% of the adults had been to France. Twice as many more had been to Spain only.

Complete the Venn diagram using the information provided.

(3)

Spain

9

France

17 (a) Sheila wants to make 30 cookies for her class mates. However, she only has the recipe to make 12. Complete the ingredients table so she can make 30.

Ingredients for 12 Cookies

120g Butter
90g Sugar
1 Egg
225g Flour
Half tsp Salt
200g Chocolate Chips

Ingredients for 30 Cookies

_____ g Butter
_____ g Sugar
3 Eggs
562.5g Flour
_____ tsp Salt
500g Chocolate Chips

(3)

(b) It takes Sheila 2 hours to clean up, how long in minutes would it take 4 people?

(1)

SCORE

7

Question	ANSWER	MARKS R	T

18 The timetable below shows the start times of all the showings at the local cinema for five different movies.

Movies	Show Times			
Warships	10:00	10:45	11:40	12:30
Monsters in the Zoo	10:05	12:00	13:15	14:40
Super Shoes	10:30	11:15	12:45	13:45
Shark Attack	09:45	11:45	14:00	16:05
Cinderella	09:15	10:00	12:20	13:50

(a) If Brenda arrives at the cinema at 10:01, how many showings will she have missed the start of?

(1)

(b) How long will she need to wait to watch the next showing of Warships?

(1)

(c) If it takes 23 minutes to get to the cinema and 10 minutes to buy the tickets, what time should Brenda have left home to watch the 12:20 showing of Cinderella?

(1)

(d) If Shark Attack lasts 2 hours and 17 minutes, what time will the second showing end?

(1)

SCORE	
	4

Question			ANSWER	MARKS R	T

19 The table below shows the minimum scores needed to join either the amber list or the green list at a choice of four grammar schools.

The required scores are lower for <u>only the school</u> where a sibling already attends.

	Sibling	Amber List	Green List
School A	Yes	303 or higher	314 or higher
	No	303 or higher	335 or higher
School B	Yes	303 or higher	319 or higher
	No	303 or higher	333 or higher
School C	Yes	310 or higher	343 or higher
	No	320 or higher	346 or higher
School D	Yes	310 or higher	347 or higher
	No	320 or higher	349 or higher

(a) Joaquim has a sibling at School B and a score of 320.
Will school B add him to the 'amber list' or 'green list'?

(1)

(b) Gary has no siblings and a score of 320.
Which schools, if any, will add him to their 'green list'?

(1)

(c) Mia has no siblings and a score of 348.
Which schools, if any, will add her only to their 'amber list'?

(1)

(d) Poppy has a sibling at School A and a score of 315.
Which schools, if any, will add her only to their 'amber list'?

(1)

(e) Trevor has no siblings. What is the highest mark he could have achieved to be on the amber list at the school C?

(1)

SCORE

5

END OF PAPER

11+ CSSE Mock

Mathematics Paper 2

60 Minutes

PAGE	SCORE	
	Marks	Total
16		6
17		9
18		4
19		5
20		6
21		3
22		6
23		6
24		6
25		5
26		4
TOT:		60

The questions in this paper are worth 60 marks

Attempt all the questions, writing your answers clearly

If you cannot answer a question, leave it and go on to the next one

Use any time you have left to check your answers and go back to any unanswered questions

The numbers in brackets are the marks available for each question

Do NOT use a calculator

Question	ANSWER	MARKS R T
1 (a) Subtract the difference between 30 and 15 from the product of 12 and 6.		(1)
(b) Add together 11.03 + 0.64 + 6.44		(1)
(c) What number must be added to 7.99 to make 11.01		(1)
2 (a) Complete the following fractions: $\dfrac{1}{3} + \dfrac{5}{\_} = \dfrac{8}{9}$		(1)
(b) Workout the following and provide the answer in simplest form: $\dfrac{1}{3} \times 2\dfrac{7}{10} =$		(1)
(c) Workout the following and provide the answer in simplest form: $\dfrac{1}{3} \div \dfrac{7}{10} =$		(1)

SCORE
6

Question	ANSWER	MARKS	
		R	T

3 Complete the following sequences:

(a) 8.5, 11, 13.5, 16, ___, 21

(1)

(b) 17.6, 16.8, ___, 15.2, 14.4, ___

(2)

4 From the numbers 23, 24, 25, 26 and 27, confirm which one is:

(a) A prime number

(1)

(b) A factor of 144

(1)

(c) A power of 3

(1)

5 (a) Convert 600 cm into m.

(1)

(b) Convert 15 cm² into mm².

(1)

(c) Convert 3 km into cm.

(1)

SCORE

9

Question	ANSWER	MARKS R	T

6   In this question you may assume the following exchange rates:
 	
     1 British pound (£) = 1.3 American dollars ($)
 	
     1 British pound (£) = 1.1 Euros (€)			

(a) I am flying to Euro Disney in France and have £300 with me to spend. How many Euros will I get?			(1)
(b) If I then flew to Florida Disney in America and had $299 to spend, how many British pounds would I have converted?			(1)
(c) How many Euro's will $299 be worth?			(1)
(d) I can buy a pair of shoes for €143 or $143. What is the difference in price in British Pounds £?			(1)

SCORE
T
4

Question	ANSWER	MARKS R	T
7 (a) Emily was watching a film. After 20 mins she had watched 25%. What is the total length of the film in hours and mins?			(1)
(b) Emily finished watching at 17:25 pm. If she had a 35 min break in the middle, what time did she start watching the film?			(1)
8 A box contains red, blue and green pens. There are twice as many green pens than red pens and five times more blue pens than green pens.			
(a) For every red pen, how many blue pens do I have?			(1)
(b) If I have four green pens, how many red pens will I have?			(1)
(c) If I have three red pens, how many pens will I have altogether?			(1)

SCORE	
	5

Question	ANSWER	MARKS R	T

9 A teacher asked her students if they like apples or oranges.
The teacher collected the following information:

19 children liked oranges
15 liked apples
2 didn't like either
30 children were asked in total

Complete the Venn diagram using this information – ensure you add labels

2

(3)

10 Write down the new coordinates of the points A, B and C if the triangle below is reflected in the x-axis.

A (__ , __)

B (__ , __)

(3)

C (__ , __)

SCORE
6

Question	ANSWER	MARKS R	T

11 The shape below is a symmetrical double headed arrow, with the arrow heads made up of identical isosceles triangles.

The arrow fits exactly inside a frame which is 8cm wide and 11cm long.

(a) Calculate the total perimeter of the double headed arrow.

(1)

(b) Calculate the area of triangle DEF.

(1)

(c) Calculate the total area of the unshaded part of the diagram.

(1)

SCORE

3

Question	ANSWER	MARKS R	T

12 Five children competed in three different races at school sports day.

The table below shows their completion time in seconds for three different races.

Name	Sack Race	Egg Race	Skipping Race
Shola	22.2	44.2	31.5
Sarah	18.1	53.4	30.6
Ibrahim	19.3	41.6	32.7
Lucy	18.7	47.9	30.6
Barry	21.7	50.2	33.1

(a) Who came last in the Sack Race?

(1)

(b) In which race did two children finish with the same time?

(1)

(c) Who won the most races?

(1)

13 In each part of the question below, write down the value on each scale that the arrow is pointing at.

(a)

0   1000.0   ml

(1)

(b)

300   450   grams

(1)

(c)

20   260.0   mm

(1)

SCORE

6

Question	ANSWER	MARKS R	T
14 In a shopping bag there are 4 apples, 6 plums and 5 oranges. Answer the questions below and express all answers in their simplest terms.			
(a) If I choose one piece of fruit at random, what is the probability that it is a plum?			(1)
(b) If I choose one piece of fruit at random, what is the probability that it is not an apple?			(1)
(c) If I eat all the apples, what is the probability of selecting a plum?			(1)
15 (a) The original price of a laptop is £800. The sale price is £600. What is the percentage discount?			(1)
(b) If I use my student card, I can get an extra 5% off the sale price. What is the updated sale price?			(1)
(c) If I pay the original price in 24 monthly instalments, what percentage of the cost do I have outstanding after 15 months?			(1)

SCORE 6

Question	ANSWER	MARKS R	T

16 A company wants to post 300 letters and 60 small parcels using the services below.

Service	Small Letters	Large Letters	Small Parcel
2nd Class	66p	£2.70	£3.20
1st Class	85p	£3.30	£3.85
Recorded Delivery	£2.25	£4.70	£4.85
Special Delivery	£6.85	£8.95	£8.95

The ratio of small to large letters is 1:2

All of the small letters are posted using the 2nd class service.

60% of the large letters are posted 1st class and the rest by Recorded Delivery.

10 small parcels are posted 2nd class with twice as many posted 1st class.

The remaining small parcels are posted using Special Delivery.

(a) What is the cost of posting the small letters?

£   (1)

(b) How much did the company spend on Recorded Deliveries?

£   (1)

(c) How much did the company spend in total?

£   (1)

17 Mike wrote down the shoe sizes of his family as follows: 8, 5, 1, 9, 3, 4

(a) What was the average (mean) shoe size?

(1)

(b) What is the median shoe size?

(1)

(c) Mike removes one number from the list so that the new average is 5.4? Which shoe size did he remove?

(1)

SCORE
6

Question	ANSWER	MARKS R	T

18 The rectangle ABCD is made up of two identical isosceles triangles, ABD and BDC with parallel lines as shown.

Calculate the angle of X and Y.

X° : _____ (1)

Y° : _____ (1)

19 Ethel sells pens for 50p each with a fixed delivery charge of £2.

(a) Is it **TRUE** or **FALSE** that the formula for calculating the cost of the pens including delivery is:

P = 50n + 2, when P = total price and n = number of pens (1)

(b) Is it **TRUE** or **FALSE** that a pack of 70 pens will cost £37? (1)

(c) Is it **TRUE** or **FALSE** that if I spent £5 then I bought 6 pens? (1)

SCORE 5

Question	ANSWER	MARKS R	T

20 The diagram below is part of the central line tube map in London.

The arrows indicate the distance between the four stations in metres.

Marble Arch   Bond St   Oxford Circus   Holborn

Tottenham

1446m

2150m

850m

(a) What is the difference in metres between Bond St and Oxford Circus stations?

(1)

(b) What is the difference in metres between Oxford Circus and Holborn stations?

(1)

(c) Tottenham is 867m away from Holborn station.
How far from Marble Arch is Tottenham in km?

(1)

(d) Using a scale of 1 cm: 300 m, how many cm apart would Marble Arch and Holborn appear on the map?

(1)

SCORE

4

END OF PAPER

Surname ....

First Name ....

Start Time: ....

End Time: ....

11+ CSSE Mock

Mathematics Paper 3

60 Minutes

The questions in this paper are worth 60 marks

Attempt all the questions, writing your answers clearly

If you cannot answer a question, leave it and go on to the next one

Use any time you have left to check your answers and go back to any unanswered questions

The numbers in brackets are the marks available for each question

Do NOT use a calculator

PAGE	SCORE	
	Marks	Total
30		7
31		9
32		4
33		5
34		5
35		5
36		4
37		6
38		7
39		5
40		3
TOT:		60

Question	ANSWER	MARKS R T
1 Find the missing numbers so that the answer is <u>always 38</u>		
(a) 50% of …….		(1)
(b) 152 divided by…….		(1)
(c) Two fifths of …….		(1)
(d) 199 minus …….		(1)
2 Here are the first five terms in a number sequence: 3, 5, 7, 9, 11		
(a) Write an expression, in terms of n, for the nth term of this number sequence.		(1)
(b) Find the 10th term in this number sequence.		(1)
(c) Work out the difference between the 1st and 20th term of the sequence.		(1)

SCORE

7

Question	ANSWER	MARKS R	T
3 In each part of the question below, write down the smallest value in the list.			
(a) 0.219 0.213 0.211 0.291 0.2915			(1)
(b) $\frac{1}{5}$ of 25 10% of 51 $\frac{1}{20}$ of 98			(1)
(c) $\frac{3}{7}$ $\frac{4}{8}$ $\frac{5}{9}$			(1)
4 The dots on the opposite faces of a dice add up to 7. Complete the net below by drawing the correct number of dots on each face.			(3)
5 (a) Convert 2.5 m into cm.			(1)
(b) Convert 0.3 km into m.			(1)
(c) Convert 200 mm into m.			(1)

SCORE	
	9

Question	ANSWER	MARKS	
		R	T

6 Ted likes to grow his own vegetables. His back garden is made up of two vegetable patches and grass. The vegetable patches are identical in size.

12m

7m

2m
Vegetable Patch 2
5m

Vegetable
Patch 1

Grass

(a) Calculate the perimeter of both vegetable patches.

(1)

(b) Calculate the area of the grass, excluding the patches.

(1)

(c) Ted lays a path 1m wide around the entire inside edge of his garden. What is the area of the path?

(1)

(d) Ted covers his path with 5kg bags of gravel.
If each bag covers 2.5 m², how many bags will he need to buy?

(1)

SCORE

4

Question	ANSWER	MARKS R	T

7 Adam finishes reading his book in one week. The number of pages he reads each day is shown on the chart below.

(a) How many pages did Adam read in total during the week?

(1)

(b) On which day did Adam read a third of the number of pages he had read on Wednesday?

(1)

(c) On which day of the week did Adam finish reading the first quarter of the book?

(1)

8 At Stratford station, trains arrive from Southend every 15 minutes, from Chelmsford every 12 minutes and from Romford every 4 minutes.
At 7am, the first train from each town arrives at Stratford station.

(a) At what time would a train from Romford and Chelmsford arrive at Stratford together again?

(1)

(b) What is the next time all three trains would arrive at Stratford together?

(1)

SCORE	
	5

Question	ANSWER	MARKS R	T

9 Katie wants to travel to Manchester from London to see her friends. She checks the train timetable and sees she has four different train times to choose from.
Note: x indicates the train does not stop at the station.

	Train 1	Train 2	Train 3	Train 4
London	09:20	09:40	10:00	10:20
Milton Keynes	09:50	x	x	10:50
Stoke	10:48	x	11:25	11:48
Crewe	x	11:11	x	x
Macclesfield	x	x	11:41	x
Wilmslow	x	11:27	x	x
Stockport	11:17	11:36	11:56	12:17
Manchester	11:27	11:46	12:05	12:27

(a) If I want to meet my friends in Manchester at 12:20, what is the latest train from London I can catch?

(1)

(b) Which train would I need to catch for the shortest journey time?

(1)

(c) How much longer does the journey take between Stoke and Stockport on Train 3 compared to Train 4?

(1)

(d) I end up catching the Train 1 at 09:20. However, my train breaks down at Stoke. How long do I wait for the next train?

(1)

(e) Train 4 returns back to London after waiting in Manchester for 30 mins. What time will Train 4 arrive back in London?

(1)

SCORE

5

Question	ANSWER	MARKS R | T

10 Eddy wants to paint his bedroom blue. Each wall has an area of 10m².
One tin of blue paint costs £15 and covers 11m².

(a) How much will Eddy need to spend to paint four walls?

(1)

(b) The store offers a 20% discount if you buy 5 tins or more.
Is it cheaper, more expensive or the same price buy 5 tins or 4?

(1)

(c) How much change will Eddy receive from £70 if he buys 5 tins?

(1)

11 The original price of a pair of jeans is £50. In the sales, they are discounted by 20%.

(a) What is the new price of the jeans in the sale?

(1)

(b) If I buy two pairs of jeans, I can get an additional 10% off the discounted price, how much will I pay in total?

(1)

SCORE 5

Question	ANSWER	MARKS R	T

12 The Table below shows the distance in kilometres between five towns.

For example, the distance between Harden and Epping is 16km.

Heaton				
7	Harden			
	16	Epping		
3	9	5	Sandy Hills	
8	18	9	2	Ascot

(a) What is the distance between Epping and Sandy Hills?

(1)

(b) If I have travelled 9km to get to Harden, where did I set off from?

(1)

(c) How many km have I travelled if I leave Heaton in the morning to travel to Ascot and then to Epping?

(1)

(d) Heaton, Harden and Epping are towns along the same Motorway in that order.
What is the distance between Heaton and Epping?

(1)

SCORE 4

Question	ANSWER	MARKS R	T

13 Shape ABCD is a parallelogram, where each line is parallel to its opposite line.

| Using the information provided, calculate angles A°, B° and C°. | A° ___ B° ___ C° ___ | | (3) |

14

(a) Which one of the following coordinates X, Y or Z is outside of the rectangle?

X (4,-4)   Y (4,-6)   Z (-6,4)

(1)

(b) Write down the coordinates of the centre of the rectangle.

(__ , __)

(1)

(c) Write down the new coordinates if point A is reflected in the Y axis.

(__ , __)

(1)

SCORE
6

37

Question	ANSWER	MARKS R	T
15 Three red bricks have a mean weight of 5kg. Five blue bricks have a mean weight of 8kg. Two green bricks have a weight of 6kg.			
(a) What is the weight of three red bricks?			(1)
(b) If four blue bricks weigh 36 kg, what is the weight of the 5th brick?			(1)
(c) What is the mean weight of all ten bricks?			(1)
16 Using only the numbers in the cloud, write down: 21 29 23 27 25			
(a) all the square numbers.			(1)
(b) all the prime numbers.			(1)
(c) all the cube numbers.			(1)
(d) any numbers that are not either a prime, cube or square number.			(1)

SCORE

7

Question	ANSWER	MARKS

<table>
<tr><td></td><td>R</td><td>T</td></tr>
</table>

17 In each of the grids below, the numbers in the four squares must be added together to give the number in the circle.

For example, 3 + 7 + 4 + 9 = 23

(a) Calculate the value of a.

(1)

(b) Calculate the value of b.

(1)

(c) Calculate values of c, d and e.

(c):

(d):

(e):

(3)

SCORE

5

39

Question	ANSWER	MARKS R	T

18 The following table shows the parking charges at a shopping mall car park.

Tariffs	
Up to 1 hour	£1.50
1-2 hours	£2.00
2-3 hours	£2.50
3-4 hours	£3.00
4-5 hours	£3.50
5-6 hours	£4.00
Over 6 hours	£8.00
Sundays	£1.50 all day

(a) How much will it cost to park for 2 hours 20 mins?

(1)

(b) If I arrived at the car park at 11:23am and left at 2:30pm, how much would I pay?

(1)

(c) If I parked for 7 hours on each day of the weekend, how much would I pay in total?

(1)

END OF PAPER

SCORE

3

11+ CSSE Mock

Mathematics Paper 4

60 Minutes

The questions in this paper are worth 60 marks

Attempt all the questions, writing your answers clearly

If you cannot answer a question, leave it and go on to the next one

Use any time you have left to check your answers and go back to any unanswered questions

The numbers in brackets are the marks available for each question

Do NOT use a calculator

PAGE	SCORE	
	Marks	Total
42		6
43		7
44		3
45		5
46		7
47		3
48		7
49		6
50		6
51		6
52		4
TOT:		60

Question	ANSWER	MARKS	
		R	T
1 (a) Write 40% as a fraction in its simplest form.			(1)
(b) Write 0.65 as a fraction in its simplest form.			(1)
(c) What is a 1/3 of a 1/5?			(1)
2 (a) Theresa cuts a 1.32kg cake into equal pieces of 110g each. How many pieces did she cut the cake into?			(1)
(b) An egg carton can hold half a dozen eggs. How many cartons will Jeremy need if he has 43 eggs?			(1)
(c) If the temperature falls to minus 6 degrees from 31 degrees, by how many degrees did the temperature fall?			(1)
		SCORE	6

Question	ANSWER	MARKS R	T
3 A class of 11+ pupils are set a maths test with 10 questions. A correct answer scores 5 marks, a wrong answer loses 3 marks and no answer scores 0 marks.			
(a) Ash answers 10 questions correctly. What is his score?			(1)
(b) Brad answers 6 questions correctly, 2 incorrect and the rest blank. What is his score?			(1)
(c) Charlie answers all the questions and scores 42 marks. How many questions did she get right?			(1)
(d) Dina got twice as many right as she got wrong and scored 21. How many answer spaces did she leave blank?			(1)
4 In the triangle shown below, angle 'A' is half the size of angle 'B' and a third the size of angle 'C'. What are the sizes of angles 'A', 'B' and 'C'?			
	A° ____ B° ____ C° ____		(3)

SCORE

7

Question	ANSWER	MARKS	
		R	T

5 Zara has plotted the location of four buildings on the graph shown below.

(a) Write down the coordinates of the mall.			(1)
(b) Which building can be rotated about the point (0, 0) to land in the same location as the Library?			(1)
(c) Zara walks in a straight line from her home to the mall. What are the coordinates of her location when exactly half way?			(1)

SCORE

3

Question	ANSWER	MARKS R	T

6 The nutritional label shown below was taken from a 30g bar of chocolate.
One milligram (mg) is one thousandth of a gram or one thousand micrograms.

NUTRITION INFORMATION

Serving Size	30 g	Carbohydrates	7 g
Calories	117	Fibre	3g
Fat	3 g	Sugar	3 g
Cholesterol	0 mg	Calcium	47 mg
Sodium	111 mg	Iron	1 mg

(a) How many grams of fat are there in 1kg of chocolate?

(1)

(b) If I don't want to exceed 300 calories of chocolate in a day, how many whole bars can I eat in a day?

(1)

(c) How many micrograms of calcium do three bars of chocolate contain?

(1)

7 Using the rule 4A = B, calculate the value of A in the following equations:

(a) 3A + 11 = B - 20

(1)

(b) AB + B² = 20

(1)

SCORE	
	5

Question	ANSWER	MARKS R	T
8 (a) 300 adults and children board a plane. If 85% of them arrived at the airport by car, how many didn't arrive by car?			(1)
(b) There are 12% more men than women on the plane. If 35% of the passengers are women. How many men are there?			(1)
(c) How many children are there?			(1)

9 Li Wei has 9 cards, each with a number on it from 1 to 9.

If he picks a card at random, what is the probability that:

1 2 3 4 5 6 7 8 9

(a) He picks an even number?			(1)
(b) A number greater than 6?			(1)
(c) A factor of 16?			(1)
(d) A prime number?			(1)

SCORE 7

Question	ANSWER	MARKS	
		R	T

10 Amy is measuring the combined weight of some parcels.

She places each parcel on the scales one by one, without removing any.

(a) What is the weight of the first parcel?

(1)

(b) What is the weight of the second parcel on its own?

(1)

(c) Amy places the third parcel on the scales. What is the combined weight of the first and third parcels only?

(1)

SCORE

3

47

Question	ANSWER	MARKS R	T

11 Bart creates a table to help memorise how to convert between different units.

For example, to convert from kg to g, you multiply by 1000, so he writes "x 1000".

Complete the missing answers in the 'How?' column.

Category	From	To	How?
Weight	kg	g	X 1000
Volume	Litre	ml	(a)
Area	km²	m²	(b)
Distance	mm	m	(c)
speed	km per hour	km per minute	(d)

(4)

12 (a) Ash drives his car 210 miles in 3 hours to Glasgow. Calculate his average speed in mph (miles per hour).

(1)

(b) Ash then travels 50 miles to Edinburgh at an average speed of 25 mph due to road works. Work out how long the journey lasts.

(1)

(c) Finally, Ash drives 7 hours to London at an average speed of 58 mph. Calculate how far he drove.

(1)

SCORE

7

48

Question	ANSWER	MARKS R	T

13 The cuboid boxes below both have the same volume, but different length, height and widths. Note the cuboids are not drawn to scale.

5m

6m

3m

Cuboid 1

10m

Xm

3m

Cuboid 2

(a) Calculate the surface area of cuboid 1.

(1)

(b) Calculate the volume of cuboid 1.

(1)

(c) Calculate the height, X, of cuboid 2.

(1)

14 Complete the three missing values in the table below.

	Edges	Faces	Vertices
Triangular Prism	a) ____	5	b) ____
Cylinder	2	c) ____	0

(3)

SCORE

6

Question	ANSWER	MARKS R	T

15 Adam and Julie count how much pocket money they save over a 100 day period. They record their savings every 10 days and plot the line graph shown below.

(a) How many £ did Julie start with at the beginning of the 100 days? | | | (1)

(b) How much had Adam saved on day 60? | | | (1)

(c) How much more did Adam save than Julie from day 60 to 80? | | | (1)

16 The dimensions of a television set are in the ratio Length: 12, Height: 8, Depth: 2
If the actual depth of the television set is 5cm, calculate:

(a) The height of the TV? | | | (1)

(b) The length of the TV? | | | (1)

(c) The combined length of all the edges of the TV? | | | (1)

SCORE	
	6

50

Question	ANSWER	MARKS R	T

17 The TV listings for two different channels are shown below. Salasi starts his evening by watching the BBC News at 18:15.

BBC 1	
BBC News	18:15
The One Show	19:25
Panorama	19:55
EastEnders	20:20
Bake Off	21:15
Casualty	22:20

ITV	
ITV News	18:00
Emmerdale	18:45
Coronation Street	19:15
You've been Framed	20:45
Football	21:25
Movie	23:35

(a) Salasi is watching the BBC news. After 50 mins he changes channel to ITV. What programme will be showing?

(1)

(b) Salasi watches all of Coronation Street. How many minutes of Bake Off are remaining for him to watch?

(1)

(c) What time will the movie on ITV end if it is 2 hours and 17 minutes long? Write your answer in 24 hour format.

(1)

18 Mr and Mrs Craig and their 2 children are travelling to London by train. A one-way adult ticket costs £18 and a child ticket is half the price of an adult ticket.

(a) How much will it cost for the Craig family to travel to London?

(1)

(b) If they use a railcard, they will save a third off <u>adult tickets only</u>. How much will they save on a return journey?

(1)

(c) What is the total cost of a two-way trip for the family with a railcard?

(1)

SCORE	
	6

Question	ANSWER	MARKS R	T

19 Mr and Mrs Harvey plan to fly on holiday with their son. The airline has a suitcase allowance of 32kg per passenger.

Passengers are also allowed an <u>additional</u> 23kg each for hand luggage.

They can have as many bags as they like, however, the total weight cannot exceed the amounts specified.

(a) What is the maximum combined suitcase and hand luggage weight the Harvey family can pack for holiday?

(1)

(b) The family suitcases can only hold a maximum of 24kg each – how many suitcases will the Harvey's need to take so that they use up all of their suitcase allowance?

(1)

(c) Mrs Harvey has 20,000g of hand luggage, Mr Harvey has 3000g and their son has 15kg of hand luggage. How much more weight can they add before using all their hand luggage allowance?

(1)

(d) Mr Harvey wants to reduce the weight of the suitcases to 16kg each because of his bad back. How many extra suitcases will he need so he still uses his maximum allowance?

(1)

SCORE 4

END OF PAPER

11+ CSSE Mock

Mathematics Paper 5

60 Minutes

The questions in this paper are worth 60 marks

Attempt all the questions, writing your answers clearly

If you cannot answer a question, leave it and go on to the next one

Use any time you have left to check your answers and go back to any unanswered questions

The numbers in brackets are the marks available for each question

Do NOT use a calculator

PAGE	SCORE	
	Marks	Total
56		6
57		7
58		6
59		5
60		4
61		6
62		6
63		6
64		5
65		5
66		4
TOT:		60

Question	ANSWER	MARKS R	T
1 Given that 22 x 15 = 330, calculate the following:			
(a) 22 x 30			(1)
(b) 330 ÷ 11			(1)
(c) 2.2 x 150			(1)
2 (a) Identify two square numbers that add up to 34. $\square^2 + \square^2$			(1)
(b) Identify a prime number and a cube number that add up to 11. $\square + \square^3$			(1)
(c) Hank's tutor asks him to write down all the prime numbers from 1 to 25. From the list below, how many has he missed? 2, 3, 7, 11, 13, 17, 19			(1)

SCORE
6

Question		ANSWER	MARKS	
			R	T

3 Shown below is a copy of Sasha's shopping bill.

Calculate the missing amounts and fill in the blank spaces.

Description	Quantity	Price per item	Total
Crisps	6	£0.70	£
Cola	6	£1.00	£6.00
Apples	5	£	£2.50
		Delivery Charge	£
		Total Bill	**£16.20**
		Amount Paid	£20.00
		Change Due	£

(4)

4 The journey planner below shows the time it takes to travel between stations.

Chelmsford — Stratford — Oxford Circus — Bakerloo — Paddington — Heathrow

27 min   19 min   8 min   8 min   16 min

(a) If I arrive at Stratford at 14:25, what time did I start my journey?

(1)

(b) How long will it take me to get from Stratford to Heathrow?

(1)

(c) What is the entire duration of my journey in hours and minutes?

(1)

SCORE

7

Question	ANSWER	MARKS R	T

5 A number of children were asked at school what their favourite pizza topping was. The pie chart and partially completed table below shows the results.

Topping	Children	Angle
Chicken	30	180°
Pineapple	3	
Sweetcorn	12	
Mushroom		90°

(a) What angle is the Sweetcorn segment?

(1)

(b) What angle is the Pineapple segment?

(1)

(c) How many children liked mushrooms?

(1)

6 The table below shows the properties of a square based pyramid and a cube. Complete the three missing values in the table below:

	Edges	Faces	Vertices
Square Based Pyramid	a) ____	5	c) ____
Cube	12	b) ____	8

(3)

SCORE
6

Question	ANSWER	MARKS R	T

7 The shape shown is made from five identical squares.

The total area of the shape is 45m².

(a) What is the area of one square?

(1)

(b) What is the length of the side marked X?

(1)

(c) Calculate the perimeter of the entire shape.

(1)

8 Two isosceles triangles have been drawn with differing angles.

(2)

(a) Calculate the size of angle A°.

(b) Calculate the size of angle B°.

SCORE

5

Question	ANSWER	MARKS R	T

9 Pogba wants to travel from Milton to Stretley to visit his friend. He has three possible routes to get to his destination, but decides to take the scenic option via Tebworth.

(a) If Pogba travels at an average speed of 40 km/h for 45 minutes, from Milton to Tebworth, how many km did he travel?

(1)

(b) Next, Pogba travels 50 km in 50 minutes to get from Tebworth to Stretley, what is his average speed?

(1)

(c) If Pogba travels from Milton to Stretley via Toddington, how long will the journey take if his average speed is 60 km/h and the distance travelled was 90km? Answer in hours and minutes.

(1)

(d) How many seconds longer will it take Pogba to travel via Tebworth to Stretley instead of via Toddington to Stretley?

(1)

SCORE

4

Question	ANSWER	MARKS R	T

10 Eve isn't feeling well today so her mum measures her body temperature at two different times using a thermometer shown below. A normal temperature is 37.5 °C.

(a) What is Eve's body temperature at 10am?

(1)

(b) By how many °C is her temperature higher than normal?

(1)

(c) What was the temperature change between 10am and 8pm?

(1)

11 There are three blackcurrant, four toffee and 5 strawberry flavoured sweets in a bag. Calculate the probability of picking:

(a) a strawberry flavoured sweet at random?

(1)

(b) a toffee or blackcurrant flavoured sweet?

(1)

(c) One blackcurrant and one strawberry sweet one after the other without replacing either back in the bag?

(1)

SCORE

6

Question	ANSWER	MARKS R	T
12 Jeremy fills his car with petrol on Monday. He spends £1.20 per litre. By Thursday he only has $\frac{1}{4}$ of a tank left. By next Monday, Jeremy again fills his tank, this time spending £1.26 per litre.			
(a) What percentage of his petrol had Jeremy used by Thursday?			(1)
(b) What was the percentage increase in petrol price after 1 week?			(1)
(c) The cost of petrol increases again by a further 10%, what is the new price of petrol rounded to the nearest pence per litre?			(1)
13 (a) Round 4.5995 to two decimal places.			(1)
(b) A school has 840 pupils. This has been rounded to the nearest 10. What is the smallest possible number of pupils?			(1)
(c) The population of Tipco is one hundred thousand, rounded to the nearest hundred thousand. What is the greatest possible number of people living in Tipco?			(1)

SCORE 6

Question	ANSWER	MARKS R	T

14 Martha has 4 numbered cards. Answer the questions by filling in the blanks.

| 8 | 2 | 5 | 3 |

(a) Rearrange the four cards to make the smallest possible number.

(1)

(b) Rearrange the cards to make the following sum true.

2 [ ] + [ ][ ] = 6 3

(1)

(c) Rearrange the cards to make the result of the subtraction as large as possible.

[ ][ ] - [ ][ ] = [ ][ ]

(1)

15 In a singing competition, four judges award marks ranging anywhere from 10 to minus 10 to each singer. There are 4 singers in total.

Singer A scored the highest possible marks from each judge.

Singer B scored 11 marks less than Person A.

Singer C and D both scored in total half the marks of Person A.

Using this information, complete the table below:

	Judge 1	Judge 2	Judge 3	Judge 4	Total
Singer A					
Singer B	7	8	6		
Singer C	6		10	9	
Singer D	8	8	-2	6	20

(3)

SCORE

6

Question	ANSWER	MARKS R	T

16 Liam completes five tests from his CSSE practice paper book.

Each paper is marked out of 60 and his scores are shown below.

	Paper 1	Paper 2	Paper 3	Paper 4	Paper 5
SCORE	26	32	49	37	41

(a) Write down the median of Liam's five scores.

(1)

(b) Write down the range of marks that Liam has achieved.

(1)

(c) What is the mean score that Liam achieved?

(1)

(d) Liam completes the final paper 6. What score did he achieve if his new mean (average) is 39?

(1)

17 By how much is 'five and a half' greater than 'three and four tenths'? Write your answer as a simplified fraction.

(1)

SCORE 5

Question	ANSWER	MARKS R	T
18 Answer the following questions:			
(a) If 10(x + 3) = 50, what is the value of x?			(1)
(b) If 2x + y + 9 + 2xy = 47, what is the value of x, if y = 2			(1)
(c) v = u + 8t. Work out t when u = 7 and v = 63			(1)
(d) Expand and simplify 3(x + 3) + 1			(1)
(e) The width of a rectangle is x and the length is x + 3 Write a simplified expression for the perimeter of the rectangle.			(1)

SCORE	
	5

Question	ANSWER	MARKS R	T

19 The grid below shows the coordinates for a kite.

(a) Write the coordinates of Point A when reflected in the Y-axis.

(1)

(b) Write the coordinates of the mid-point between B and C.

(1)

(c) Write the coordinates of Point B when rotated 270° clockwise.

(1)

(d) Write the coordinates of Point C when reflected in the X-axis
and then rotated 90° anti-clockwise.

(1)

END OF PAPER

SCORE
4

11+ CSSE Mock

Mathematics Paper 6

60 Minutes

The questions in this paper are worth 60 marks

Attempt all the questions, writing your answers clearly

If you cannot answer a question, leave it and go on to the next one

Use any time you have left to check your answers and go back to any unanswered questions

The numbers in brackets are the marks available for each question

Do NOT use a calculator

PAGE	SCORE	
	Marks	Total
68		5
69		4
70		6
71		7
72		6
73		4
74		3
75		5
76		6
77		5
78		3
79		6
TOT:		60

Question	ANSWER	MARKS	
		R	T
1 (a) Calculate: 593 + 1377			(1)
(b) Calculate: 0.6 + 669 + 0.9006			(1)
(c) Calculate: 0.6 ÷ 3			(1)
(d) Calculate: $6\frac{1}{2} + 5\frac{2}{7}$			(1)
(e) Calculate: 49 ÷ 7			(1)

SCORE
5

Question	ANSWER	MARKS
		R | T

2 Timmy completed the n rule table below for his homework. However, his little sister rubbed out some of his work.

Complete the two missing values in the table in the gaps provided.

n	5n + ___
1	6
2	11
3	16
4	___
5	26

(2)

3 (a) What is the smallest angle between the hour hand and the minute hand of a clock, at 7pm?

° (1)

(b) What is the largest angle between the hour hand and the minute hand of a clock, at 4:30am?

° (1)

SCORE

4

69

Question	ANSWER	MARKS R	T

4 Sara starts to plot four points, A, B, C and D of a parallelogram on a chart, however, misses the fourth coordinate D.

(a) Complete the fourth coordinate, D.

$(\_\_ , 6)$ (1)

(b) If point B is reflected in the x-axis, what will be its new coordinates?

$(\_\_ , \_\_)$ (1)

(c) If point A is rotated 270 degrees anti-clockwise around point (0,0), what will be its new coordinates?

$(\_\_ , \_\_)$ (1)

5 Beatrice completes an 11+ practice paper each day of a particular week. Her percentage scores are recorded in the table below:

Test Paper	Test 1	Test 2	Test 3	Test 4	Test 5
Score	60%	53%	46%	77%	?

(a) If the average is 65%, calculate what the score was for Test 5? (1)

(b) What is the range of scores from Test 1 to Test 5? (1)

(c) What is the median score from Test 1 to Test 5? (1)

SCORE 6

70

Question	ANSWER	MARKS R	T

6 From the list of numbers below:

1, 9, 13, 17, 19, 25, 31, 77

(a) What fraction are Prime numbers? — (1)

(b) What fraction are Square numbers? — (1)

(c) What is 4^3? — (1)

(d) Is the number 4^3 larger, smaller or equal to 8^2? — (1)

7 The table below shows the average highest and lowest temperatures in London last year, together with the average number of days it rained in each month.

	Jan	Feb	Mar	Apr	May	Jun	Jul	Aug	Sep	Oct	Nov	Dec
High °C	6	7	10	13	17	20	22	21	19	14	10	7
Low °C	3	3	4	6	9	12	14	14	12	9	6	3
Days Rain	11	9	9	9	9	7	6	6	7	10	10	10

(a) What is the difference between the highest and lowest temperature of the year? — (1)

(b) Which month has the smallest difference between its highest and lowest temperature? — (1)

(c) If I wanted to travel to London when it rained no more than eight days in a month and the average temperature is no higher than 20°C, then in which two months should I travel? — (1)

SCORE 7

71

Question	ANSWER	MARKS R	T
8 Maizy and Daisy are playing a maths game. Maizy shouts out a number, Daisy doubles it and adds 15 then and writes down the answer.			
(a) When Maizy calls out "45", what does Daisy write down?			(1)
(b) If Daisy wrote down "25", what number did Maizy call out?			(1)
(c) When Maizy calls out "minus 5.5", what does Daisy write down?			(1)
9 If the following numbers were placed in increasing order: $\frac{4}{5}$, $\frac{2}{3}$, 70%, 0.75, $\frac{9}{10}$			
(a) Which number would be in the middle?			(1)
(b) Which value would come immediately before 0.75?			(1)
(c) If 0.75 has been rounded up to two decimal places, what is the smallest 3 decimal place number it could have been?			(1)

SCORE
6

Question	ANSWER	MARKS R	T

10 North Girls School entered into a maths test against East Boys School

The results of the competition are shown below:

Students Total	Passed	Failed
240 Girls	180	60
160 Boys	120	40

(a) What percentage of girls failed out of the 240 girls that entered?

(1)

(b) What percentage of boys passed out of the total number of candidates that entered from <u>both</u> schools?

(1)

(c) The trophy was awarded to the school with the highest percentage pass rate – who won the trophy, Girls, Boys or draw?

(1)

(d) If the results of half of the failed boys are changed to a pass, what would be the new percentage pass rate for the boy's school?

(1)

SCORE

4

Question	ANSWER	MARKS R	T

11 Name the shape that will be created for each of the 3D nets below:

(a) Shape 1

(1)

(b) Shape 2

(1)

(c) Shape 3

(1)

SCORE 3

Question	ANSWER	MARKS R	T

12 Mum and Dad weigh themselves on a scale. Write down their weight in KG indicated by the pointer.

(a) Dad

76.3   77.0

(1)

(b) Mum

67.2   67.9

(1)

(c) On the scale below, draw an arrow to indicate a weight of 88.55

88.5   88.7

(1)

13 (a) Add together the four lengths of 1.5m, 1200mm, 5cm and 0.01km. Provide your answer in cm.

(1)

(b) A large bottle weighs 0.7kg. If I empty half the bottle, it weighs 0.4 kg. What is the weight of the empty bottle alone?

(1)

SCORE 5

Question	ANSWER	MARKS R	T
14 (a) Is it **TRUE** or **FALSE** that Speed = Distance x Time?			(1)
(b) Is it **TRUE** or **FALSE** that a speed of 10 miles per hour is the equivalent of 600 miles per minute?			(1)
(c) Is it **TRUE** or **FALSE** that a speed of 120 miles per hour means I will have travelled 100 miles in 50 minutes?			(1)

15 In the parallelogram shown below, length AD is 9 cm and BE is 7 cm.

Question	ANSWER	MARKS R	T
(a) Calculate in cm², the area of parallelogram ABCD.			(1)
(b) What is the perimeter of shape ABDC in cm?			(1)
(c) Calculate the area of triangle CDE in cm.			(1)

SCORE

6

76

Question	ANSWER	MARKS R | T

16 60 children took part in a vote for their favourite cartoon from a list of 5 choices.

The pie chart shows the results of the vote.

Pie chart sections: Scooby Doo 54°, Winx Club, Mr Bean 120°, Tom & Jerry, Larva Island (with right angle marked).

(a) If 20% of the children voted for Tom & Jerry, what angle in degrees would the "Tom and Jerry" section represent? (1)

(b) What angle should the "Winx Club" section represent? (1)

(c) How many children voted for Larva Island? (1)

(d) How many children didn't vote for Mr Bean and Larva Island? (1)

(e) How many degrees does one child represent in the pie chart? (1)

SCORE 5

77

Question	ANSWER	MARKS R	T
17 (a) Andy's mum wakes him up eight minutes before 8am to get ready for school. It takes him seventeen minutes to get out of bed. What time did Andy finally wake up? Specify am or pm.			(1)
(b) It takes Andy 19 minutes to get ready and then 16 minutes to walk to school. What time does he arrive at school?			(1)
(c) If school finishes at 2:55pm, how long will Andy have been at school for the day?			(1)
18 (a) My moneybox has £4.00 made up of only 10p, 20p and 50p coins. If I have three 10p coins and twice as many 20p coins, then how many 50p coins will I have?			(1)
(b) Using my £4.00, I buy 2 packets of sweets for a total of 80p. How much money will I have left over?			(1)
(c) How many more packets of sweets can I buy with my leftover money?			(1)

SCORE
6

Question	ANSWER	MARKS	
		R	T

19 A box contains three flavours of crisps: 'Cheese', 'Salted' and 'Prawn' in the ratio 1:2:3. If there are 48 packets of crisp in the box:

(a) How many are 'Cheese' flavoured?

(1)

(b) How many are 'Salted' flavoured?

(1)

(c) If I eat half of the Prawn flavoured crisps, how many packets of crisps will I have left in the whole box?

(1)

END OF PAPER

SCORE	
	3

ANSWER
SECTION

Qn	Part	Answer	Explain
1	a	6.1	Add numbers together and ÷ 2 to find halfway mark
	b	5	Add numbers together and ÷ 2 to find halfway mark
2	a	49	Numbers increase by 9
	b	6.5	Numbers increase by 0.75
	c	12.5	Numbers decrease by 10.5
3	a	2700 g	3000g - 300
	b	5.63 Kg	5750 - 120
	c	0.42 Kg	10p = 7g, so £1 = 70g
4	a	9	95 – 32 = 63 x 5 = 315 315 ÷ 35 = 9
	b	212 ºF	100 x 9 =900 ÷ 5 = 180 180 + 32 = 212
5	a	A (-4, 20) B (16, 16) C (-8, 0)	Calculate the length and base by subtracting the x and y coordinates Base of each triangle is 4 (0- -4) Length of each triangle is 16 (12 + 4)
	d	(-16, 16)	
6	a	44.44%	Increase from Jan to Fen = 3,900 – 2,700 = 1,200 1,200 ÷ 2,700 = 44.44
	b	88%	3,432 ÷ 3900 = 0.88 x 100 = 88
	c	65 million	6% = 3,900,000 therefore 1% = 650,000 100% = 65,000,000
	d	150,000	Jan in Wales is 162,000 which is 8% higher than Dec (162 ÷ 108%) x 100 = 150
	e	525,000	7/8 have symptoms therefore 1/8 don't 1/8 x 4,200,000 = 525,000
7	a	10	A quarter of 40 is 10, so 30 remaining
	b	24	A fifth of 30 - eats 6, so 24 remaining
	c	12	A half of 24
8	a	44°	180° – 90° (right angle) - 46°
	b	90°	180° - 60° = 120°, 120 ÷ 4 = 30°, therefore 3 x 30° = 90°
	c	00:25	5 min = 30°, 150° = 25mins - large hand means movement in mins

Qn	Part	Answer	Explain
9	a	£31.98	2 Child x 4.99 = £9.98 + 4 Student x £3.25 = £13 3D Movie = 6 tickets x £1.50 = £9
	b	£4	Only the Child ticket is more expensive by £2 £2 x 2 tickets = £4
	c	6 tickets	47.94 ÷ 7.99. Note the cost is not divisible by £10, so cannot have been the afternoon ticket.
10	a	21°	126 ÷ 6
	b	28°	(22 x 7) - 126
11	a		
	b		
	c		
12	a	25 kg	
	b	13.5 kg	Increases in units of 1.5kg
	c	17.5 kg	Each major unit is 5kg, therefore half unit is 2.5kg
13	a	112 km	1.6 x 70 = 112
	b	340.6 km	31 miles x 1.6 = 49.6km + 291km
	c	565.75 miles	(a) + (b) = 452.6km one way, x2 = 905.2 905.2 ÷ 1.6 = 565.75 miles
14	a	4 Pairs	13 + 23 = 36, 17 + 19 = 36 5 + 31 = 36, 29 + 7 = 36
15	a	198 cm²	(3 x 9) + (3 x 6) + (9 x 6) x 2
	b	162 cm³	9 x 3 x 6
	c	108 cm³	Two thirds x 162
	d	1 jug	8 x 162 = 1.296l, i.e. 1.2 jugs, or 1 full jug
16			22% of 50 adults = 11 had been to France. 11 – 9 already populated in the 'both' section = 2
			Twice as many adults went to Spain only Therefore, 2 x 11 = 22
			No countries = 50 – 22 – 9 – 2 = 17

Qn	Part	Answer	Explain
17	a	300 g	12 cookies 120g, therefore 3 cookies is 30g
		225 g	12 cookies 90g, therefore 3 cookies is 22.5g
		1 and 1/4 tsp	0.5 tsp for 12 cookies, so 0.25 for 6 and 0.125 for 3 cookies
	b	30 mins	2 hours' worth of work for 1 person. 120min ÷ 4
18	a	4	Warships at 10am and Shark Attack 9:45 were both missed. Two showings of Cinderella started before 10:01
	b	44 min	10:01 to 10:45 - a 44 min wait
	c	11:47	12:20 less 33 mins
	d	14:02	Second showing is 11:45, + 2 hours 17 min
19	a	Green List	A score of 319 or above is required if you have a sibling at school B
	b	No School	All scores needed without a sibling are higher than 320
	c	School D	Because score needed is 349 or higher
	d	School B	School A (with sibling) will add to her to the green list. School B (no sibling) will add to amber list School C & D (no sibling) – score is too low to make either list
	e	345	Anything higher than 345 would mean be on the green list

Qn	Part	Answer	Explain
1	a	57	(12 x 6) - (30-15)
	b	18.11	11.03 + 0.64 + 6.44
	c	3.02	11.01 - 7.99
2	a	$\frac{5}{9}$	Convert all the denominators to 9
	b	$\frac{9}{10}$	27/30
	c	$\frac{10}{21}$	
3	a	18.5	Each number increases by 2.5
	b	16 and 13.6	Each number decreases by 0.8
4	a	23	23 is prime number
	b	24	24 x 6 = 144, therefore a factor
	c	27	3 x 3 x 3 = 27, a cube number
5	a	6 m	
	b	1500 mm²	
	c	300,000 cm	
6	a	€ 330	300 x 1.1
	b	£230	299 ÷ 1.3
	c	£253	£230 x 1.1
	d	£20	(143 ÷ 1.1) - (143 ÷ 1.3)
7	a	1 hr 20 min	25% is 20 mins, therefore 100% is 80 min
	b	3:30pm	80min + 35min = 115 min duration, i.e. 1hr 55 min. Therefore, 115m before 17:25 is 15:30
8	a	10	Ratio is Red 1: Blue 10 : Green 2
	b	2	Ratio is Red 2: Blue 20 : Green 4
	c	39	Ratio is Red 3: Blue 30 : Green 6 - total 39

Qn	Part	Answer	Explain
9	a	6 Oranges & Apples	30 - 2 - 19 - 15
9	b	13 Oranges only	19 - 6
9	c	9 Apples only	15 - 6
10	a	(-6, -3)	**Rule**: When reflecting a coordinate in the x-axis, keep the x-coordinate the same, but flip the sign of the y-coordinate.
10	b	(4, -8)	Original coordinates are (-6,3), (4,8) and (6,-4)
10	c	(6, 4)	
11	a	46 cm	10 sides in total - (4x6) + (4x3) + (2x5)
11	b	12 cm²	B to E = 11cm, DF = 8cm. Base = (11-5)/2 = 3. Answer = Half x 3 x 8cm
11	c	54 cm²	Area of frame = (11 x 8) - Area of Arrow = (5 x 2) + (12 x 2)
12	a	Shola	
12	b	Skipping	Sarah and Lucy finished with the same time of 30.6
12	c	Sarah	Sarah came first in the sack and joint first in skipping races
13	a	375 ml	1000 ÷ 8 segments. Multiply by 3
13	b	600 g	Each block of 3 segments increases by 150g
13	c	140 mm	Half way between 260 and 20 (or each segment increment is 30)
14	a	2/5	6 out of 15, simples to 2 out of 5
14	b	11/15	1 - 4/15
14	c	6/11	11 fruit left, 6 plums to choose from
15	a	25%	200 / 800
15	b	£570.00	5% of 600 = £30, so new sale price is £570
15	c	37.5%	9 out of 24 months remaining = 9/24 x 100 = 37.5%
16	a	£66	Ratio of small letters is 1:2, therefore 100 small letters. All are posted 2nd class, 100 x 66p
16	b	£376	40% of 300 = large letters = 0.4 x 200 = 80. 80 x £4.70 = £376

For question 9, a Venn diagram shows two overlapping circles: Oranges (13), overlap (6), Apples (9).

Qn	Part	Answer	Explain
	c	£1215.70	60% of 200 lrg letters 1st class = (60% x 200) x £3.30 = £396 10 sml parcels 2nd class = 10 x £3.20 = £32.00 20 sml parcels 1st class = 20 x £3.85 = £77 30 remaining parcels Special Delivery = 30 x £8.95 = £268.50 Total cost = Ans (a) + Ans (b) + £396 + £32 + £77 + £268.50 = £1,215.50
17	a	5	sum numbers and divide by 6
	b	4.5	As even list of numbers, select 2 middle numbers and average
	c	3	Multiply new average 5.4 by 5, then remove this number from sum of original i.e., 30 - 27
18	a	125°	Angle EFC = 35°, ECF = 90° therefore FEC = 180 − 125 = 55° BEF = 180° - 55° = 125°
	b	110°	180° - 35° - 35°
19	b	FALSE	Money units need to be the same, so 0.5n not 50n
	c	TRUE	70 x 0.5 + £2
	d	TRUE	6 x 0.5 + £2
20	a	596 m	1446 - 850
	b	1554 m	2150 - 596
	c	2.133 km	3000 - 867
	d	10 cm	3000 ÷ 300

Qn	Part	Answer	Explain
1	a	76	Reverse the functions - 38 x 2
	b	4	Reverse the functions - 152 ÷ 38
	c	95	Reverse the functions - 38 ÷ 0.4
	d	161	Reverse the functions - 199 - 38
2	a	2n + 1	
	b	21	2 x 10 + 1
	c	38	1st: 3, 20th: 41
3	a	0.211	
	b	1/20 of 98	
	c	3 / 7	3/7 is less than a half, 5/9 is more than a half
4			
5	a	250 cm	
	b	300 m	
	c	0.2 m	
6	a	28 m	2m + 2m + 5m + 5m = 1 patch Multiple by 2 = 28m
	b	64 m²	Area of patches = (2 x 5) x 2 = 20 m² (12 x 7) − 20 = 64
	c	34 m²	Calc area of inner rectangle and subtract from outer rectangle (12 x 7) - (5 x 10)
	d	14 bags	34 ÷ 2.5 = 13.6 bags However, can only buy whole bags, therefore round up to 14
7	a	46	5, 3, 9, 2, 4, 11, 12
	b	Tuesday	On Weds read 9, of which 1/3 is 3
	c	Wednesday	1/4 of 46 is 11.5, which falls on Weds, when he read from pages 9 to 17
8	a	7:12 AM	4 is a factor of both 4 and 12
	b	8:00 AM	60 is the next common factor between 4, 12 and 15

Qn	Part	Answer	Explain
9	a	10am / Train 3	
	b	Train 3	Train 1: 2hr 7m, Train 2: 2hr 6m, Train 3: 2hr 5m, Train 4: 2hr 7m
	c	2 mins	Train 3 takes 31min, Train 4 takes 29 min
	d	37 min	10:48 to 11:25
	e	15:04 or 3:04pm	Arrives Manchester at 2:27 + 30min wait + 2hr 07min return journey time
10	a	£60	4 tins
	b	Same price	5 x 15 = £75, less 20% at £15 is £60
	C	£10	70 - 60
11	a	£40	20% off £50 = £10
	b	£72	10% off £80 = £8
12	a	5 km	
	b	Sandy Hills	
	c	17 km	Heaton to Ascot = 8km Ascot to Epping = 9km
	d	23 km	Heaton to Harden = 7km, Harden to Epping = 16km Therefore, Heaton to Epping is 7 + 16 = 23km
13	a	110°	Angle C = Angle D because parallel lines crossing same horizontal
	b	40°	70 - 30
	c	110°	Opposite angles are equal
14	a	Y	
	b	(-1 , 1)	count halfway between the X values and then the Y values
	c	(6 , 6)	Reflect in vertical Y-axis
15	a	15 kg	3 bricks x 5kg = 15kg
	b	4 kg	Total weight = 5 bricks x 8kg = 40kg 40 kg – 36kg = 4kg
	c	6.7 kg	(3 x 5) + (5 x 8) + (2 x 6) = 15 + 40 + 12 = 67kg Therefore 67 / 10 = 6.7kg

Qn	Part	Answer	Explain
16	a	25	
	b	23 and 29	
	c	27	
	d	21	
17	a	25	1 + 7 + 11 + 6
	b	12	10 - 0.5 - 2.5 + 5
	c	1	36 - 2 - 19 - 14
	d	27	19 + 1 + 3 + 4
	e	9	23 - 3 -7 - 4
18	a	£2.50	
	b	£3.00	3hr and 7 min duration
	c	£9.50	£8 and £1.50

Qn	Part	Answer	Explain
1	a	2 / 5	40 / 100
	b	13 / 20	65 / 100
	c	1 / 15	1/3 x 1/5
2	a	12	1320 ÷ 110
	b	8	7 cartons will fit 42 eggs, so 8 needed
	c	37°	31 + 6. Do not subtract 6 from 31
3	a	50	10 x 5
	b	24	(6 x 5) - (2 x 3)
	c	9	Max score = 50 marks. 9 correct (45), 1 wrong (-3)
	d	1	6 correct (30), 3 wrong (-9), 1 blank (0)
4	a	$A = 30°$	$A + B + C = 180°$
	b	$B = 60°$	Use algebra, to replace A and B with C $\frac{1}{3}C + \frac{2}{3}C + C = 180°$
	c	$C = 90°$	$2C = 180°$ therefore $C = 90°$, $A = 30°$ and $B = 60°$
5	a	(1, -8)	
	b	The School	The school can be rotated 90° anti-clockwise from the coordinates (-4, 6) to (-6,-4)
	c	(3, -1.5)	X Coordinate is half way between the points 1 and 5 = 3 Y Coordinate is half way between the points 5 and -8 = -
6	a	100 g	30g of chocolate contains 3g fat i.e.,10%
	b	2 bars	3 bars would exceed 300 calories
	c	141,000 micrograms Do not accept 141 mg	1 bar = 47mg x 3 bars = 141mg 1mg = 1000 micrograms as stated in the question.
7	a	A = 31	3a + 11 = 4a -20 A = 11 + 20
	b	A = 1	$4(4A) + (4A)^2 = 20$ $4A^2 + 16A^2 = 20$, therefore $20A^2 = 20$, $A^2 = 1$
8	a	45	15% of 300
	b	141	35% + 12% = men, 47% of 300
	c	54	100% - 47% - 35% = 18%

Qn	Part	Answer	Explain
9	a	4 / 9	2, 4, 6, 8
	b	1 / 3	7, 8, 9 = 3 / 9
	c	4 / 9	1, 2, 4, 8 = 4 / 9
	d	4 / 9	2, 3 , 5 , 7 = 4 / 9
10	a	1.7 kg	
	b	1.6 kg	3.3 - 1.7
	c	3.2 kg	(4.8 - 3.3) is third parcel + 1.7 from first parcel
11	a	x 1000	Volume - Litre to ml
	b	x 1,000,000	Area - km² to m²
	c	÷ 1000	Distance - mm to m
	d	÷ 60	Speed - km/hour to km per min
12	a	70 mph	speed = distance ÷ time
	b	2 hours	time = distance ÷ speed
	c	406 miles	distance = speed x time
13	a	126 m²	(5 x 6 x 2) + (3 x 5 x 2) + (3 x 6 x 2) = 60 + 30 + 36
	b	90 m³	3 x 5 x 6
	c	3 m	90 ÷ 10 ÷ 3
14	a	9	edges
	b	3	faces
	c	6	vertices
15	a	£15	
	b	£60	
	c	£10	Julie: 55 - 45 = 10, Adam 80 - 60 = 20

Qn	Part	Answer	Explain
16	a	20 cm	Using ratio, the height is 4x larger than depth
	b	30 cm	Using ratio, the length is 6x larger than depth
	c	220 cm	There are 12 edges on the TV, 4 of each L, H and D Use answers from (a) + (b) + 5cm depth multiplied by 4
17	a	Emmerdale	Salasi will switch channels at 19:05
	b	30 min	Coronation street finishes 20:45, Bake-off finishes 21:15
	c	01:52	23:35 + 2hr 17
18	a	£54	2 x £18 + £9 + £9
	b	£24	(2 adults x £18) = £36, a third off 36 = £12 discount one way Therefore, both directions will be a £24 save
	c	£84	Multiply prices by 2 for return trip: Adult 24 x 2 + Child 18 x 2
19	a	165 kg	Each passenger can take a total of 55kg each and 3 passengers
	b	4 suitcases	Suitcase allowance = 32kg x 3 = 96kg. 96 ÷ 24 = 4
	c	31kg	Hand allowance = 23kg x 3 = 69kg. 69 - 20 - 3 - 15
	d	2	96kg / 16kg = 6 suitcases needed in total, They have 4 already, so 2 extra needed to reach 6

Qn	Part	Answer	Explain
1	a	660	
	b	30	
	c	330	
2	a	$5^2 + 3^2$	List of numbers to choose from up to 34 are 1, 4, 9, 16, 25
	b	3 and 2^3	List of Primes to choose from up to 11 are 2, 3, 5, 7, 11 Cube numbers up to 11 are 1 and 8
	c	2 numbers missing	5 and 23 are missing
3	Table	£4.20	Crisps: 6 x 0.70
		£0.50	Apples: 2.5 ÷ 5
		£3.50	Delivery Charge: 16.2 - 2.5 - 6 - 4.2
		£3.80	Change Due: 20 - 16.2
4	a	13:58	14.25 - 27
	b	51 mins	19 + 8 + 8 + 16
	c	1hour 18 mins	51 + 27 = 78 min
5	a	72°	From the chicken section, we can calculate that each child is equivalent to 6°. Use this information to answer all three questions
	b	18°	
	c	15 children	
6	a	8	edges
	b	6	faces
	c	5	vertices
7	a	9 m²	5 squares = 45 m² therefore 1 square = 9 m² (45 ÷ 5) One side is 3 m² (3 x 3 = 9)
	b	3 m	
	c	36 m	12 sides, 3 m each
8	a	50°	180 - 65 - 65
	b	40°	180 - (2 x A), then divide answer by 2 to get B

Qn	Part	Answer	Explain
9	a	30 km	distance = speed x time = 40 x 0.75
	b	60 km per hour	50 km in 50 min, so 1km per 1 min
	c	1 hour 30 mins	time - 90 ÷ 60 = 1.5hours
	d	300 seconds	Tebworth time is 95 mins (a) 45 + (b) 50 Toddington is 90 mins (c) 5 mins longer: 5 x 60 =
10	a	37.7 °C	
	b	0.2 °C	37.7 - 37.5
	c	- 1.1 °C	37.7 - 36.6
11	a	$\frac{5}{12}$	5/12
	b	$\frac{7}{12}$	4/12 + 3/12
	c	$\frac{15}{132}$ (or simplified $\frac{5}{44}$)	3/12 and 5/11 - multiply fractions = 15 / 132 or 5 / 44
12	a	75%	he has used 3/4 of a tank
	b	5%	6 / 120
	c	£1.39	10% = 0.126, add this to £1.26 and round = 1.386
13	a	4.60	
	b	835	834 would be rounded to 830, 835 rounds up to 840 to nearest 10
	c	149,999	150,000 would be rounded up to 200,000. 149,999 rounded down to 100,000
14	a	2 3 5 8	Arrange in ascending order to create the smallest number
	b	28+35 OR 25+38	There are TWO correct answers
	c	8 5 - 2 3 = 6 2	Create the largest number possible and subtract the smallest number possible
15	a	10, 10, 10, 10, 40	Singer A: 10 is the highest possible mark. Therefore 4 x 10 = 40
	b	8, 29	Singer B: 40 - 11 = total score of 29. 29 – 7 – 8 – 6 = 8
	c	-5,20	Singer C: Half the marks of singer A are 20 However current total is 25, therefore judge 2 awards -5

Qn	Part	Answer	Explain
16	a	37	Arrange in ascending order and select middle number
	b	23	Range is from 49 to 26
	c	37	Total of 185 ÷ 5
	d	49	(39 x 6) = 234 234 – 185 =49
17	c	2 and $\frac{1}{10}$	5.5 - 3.4 - convert to tenths, 5 tenths minus 4 tenths
18	a	x = 2	10x + 30 = 50
	b	x = 6	2x + 11 + 4x = 47 6x = 36
	c	t = 7	63 = 7 + 8t, 8t = 54, t = 7
	d	3x + 10	3x + 3x3 + 1
	e	4x + 6	(x + 3) + (x + 3) + x + x
19	a	(-3, 3)	
	b	(3, 2)	
	c	(-2, 4)	270° clockwise is the same as 90° anti-clockwise
	d	(2, 2)	

PAPER 06 ANSWERS

Qn	Part	Answer	Explain
1	a	1970	593 + 1377
	b	670.5006	0.6 + 669 + 0.9006
	c	0.2	0.6 ÷ 3
	d	$11\frac{11}{14}$	Convert the fractions to 7/14 and 4/14 to give 11/14
	e	7	49 ÷ 7
2	a	5n + 1	Pattern in each row is n multiplied by 5 + 1
	b	21	(5 x 5) + 1
3	a	150°	1 hour is equivalent to 30 degrees. Multiply by 5 hours
	b	300° (or 315°)	One hand will be on 4 and the other on 6: 2 x 30° = 60° However, largest angle is asked for: 360 – 60 = 300
4	a	(8,6) or (-4,6)	Either answer is correct
	b	(2,-6)	Reflect in horizontal x-axis
	c	(2, 2)	
5	a	89%	test 5 = (65% x number of tests) - 236
	b	43	Difference between highest and lowest numbers, 89 and 46
	c	60%	Sort all the numbers in order and select the middle number
6	a	1/2	Prime numbers are 13,17,19,31 i.e. 4 out of 8
	b	3/8	Square numbers are 1,9 and 25 i.e. 3 out of 8
	c	64	4 x 4 x 4
	d	Equal	both numbers equate to 64
7	a	19	highest 22, lowest 3
	b	January	
	c	June and Sept	June to Sept rained less than 8 days Cannot be July or Aug because both were over 20 degrees
8	a	105	45 x 2 + 15
	b	5	Reverse the equation i.e. (25 - 15) ÷ 2
	c	4	-5.5 x 2 = -11, then -11 + 15 = 4

Qn	Part	Answer	Explain
9	a	0.75	Sort all the numbers by converting all to fractions or decimals
	b	70%	
	c	0.745	Any number smaller than 0.745 would be rounded to 0.74
10	a	25%	60 ÷ 240
	b	30%	120 passed out of a total of 400 candidates
	c	Draw	Both schools achieved a 75% pass mark
	d	87.5%	Boys passed would increase from 120 to 140 from a total of 160
11	a	Hexagonal Prism	
	b	Square Based Pyramid	
	c	Cylinder	
12	a	76.75 kg	Each segment is 0.1kg
	b	67.6	Each segment is 0.1kg
	c		88.7 - 88.5 = 0.2 for 4 segments, so 1 segment is 0.05
13	a	1275 cm	convert all values to cm: 150cm + 120cm + 5cm + 1000cm Note: 0.01km = 1000cm
	b	0.1 kg	0.7 - 0.4 = 0.3kg (weight of half drink), therefore full = 0.6 kg 07 - 0.6 = 0.1 kg
14	a	FALSE	Speed = Distance ÷ Time
	b	FALSE	10 miles per hour is 10 miles per 60 minutes.
	c	TRUE	Calculate what fraction of 60 mins is 50 mins and multiply by 120
15	a	38.7 cm²	9 x 4.3 Note, there is no need to work out area of triangles separately
	b	28cm	9 + 9 + 5 + 5. Note, 7cm is the length for BE
	c	4.3 cm²	(Height 4.3cm x Base 2cm) ÷ 2

Qn	Part	Answer	Explain
16	a	72°	20% of 360 degrees
	b	24°	360 - 120 - 90 -72 - 54
	c	15	A quarter of 60 children
	d	25	Larva = 15, Mr Bean = 20, therefore 60-15-20
	e	6°	360° ÷ 60
17	a	8:09 AM	7:52 + 17m min = 8:09
	b	8:44 AM	19 + 16 = 35min. Therefore, 8:09 + 35min
	c	6 hours and 11 min	8:44 to 2:55pm (can be split into 16min + 5hr + 55min), 5hrs and 71min
18	a	5 coins	3x10p + 6 x20p = £1.50, leaving £2.50 in 50p coins
	b	£3.20	£4 - £0.80
	c	8	£3.20 ÷ cost per pack of £0.40 = 8 Answer is NOT 4 because part b states 2 packs cost 80p
19	a	8	(1/6) x 48
	b	16	(2/6) x 48
	c	36	24 prawns if halved are 12. 48 less 12

SCORECARD MATRIX

Enter Scores for each Question

	Topic	Paper 1 Qn No.	Paper 1 Score	Paper 1 Total	Paper 2 Qn No.	Paper 2 Score	Paper 2 Total	Paper 3 Qn No.	Paper 3 Score	Paper 3 Total	Paper 4 Qn No.	Paper 4 Score	Paper 4 Total	Paper 5 Qn No.	Paper 5 Score	Paper 5 Total	Paper 6 Qn No.	Paper 6 Score	Paper 6 Total	TOTALS Marks	TOTALS Total	% Correct
A	Four Rules / BODMAS	1		(2)	1		(3)	1		(4)	2		(3)	1		(3)	1		(5)		(20)	
B	Fractions	7		(3)	2		(3)	n/a	X	(0)	1		(3)	17		(1)	n/a	X	(0)		(10)	
C	Algebra, Nth Rule	n/a	X	(0)	19		(3)	2		(3)	7		(2)	18		(5)	2		(2)		(15)	
D	Angles	8		(3)	18		(2)	13		(3)	4		(3)	8		(2)	3		(2)		(15)	
E	Co-ordinates and Transformations	5		(4)	10		(3)	14		(3)	5		(3)	19		(4)	4		(3)		(20)	
F	Mean, Median and Range	10		(2)	17		(3)	15		(3)	n/a	X	(0)	16		(4)	5		(3)		(15)	
G	Square, Cube and Prime numbers	14		(1)	4		(3)	16		(4)	n/a	X	(0)	2		(3)	6		(4)		(15)	
H	Tables and Data Interpretation	19		(5)	12		(3)	18		(3)	6		(3)	15		(3)	7		(3)		(20)	
I	Number Problems (machines, missing)	4		(2)	16		(3)	17		(5)	3		(4)	14		(3)	8		(3)		(20)	
J	Ordering and Rounding Numbers	2		(3)	3		(3)	3		(3)	n/a	X	(0)	13		(3)	9		(3)		(15)	
K	Percentages	6		(5)	15		(3)	11		(2)	8		(3)	18		(3)	10		(4)		(20)	
L	Nets and Shapes	11		(3)	n/a	X	(0)	4		(3)	14		(3)	6		(3)	11		(3)		(15)	
M	Probability	n/a	X	(0)	14		(3)	n/a	X	(0)	9		(4)	11		(3)	n/a	X	(0)		(10)	
N	Reading Scales	12		(3)	13		(3)	n/a	X	(0)	10		(3)	10		(3)	12		(3)		(15)	
O	Converting Units	13		(3)	5		(3)	5	X	(3)	11		(4)	n/a	X	(0)	13		(2)		(15)	
P	Speed, Distance, Time	n/a	X	(0)	n/a	X	(0)	n/a	X	(0)	12		(3)	9		(4)	14		(3)		(10)	
Q	Area, Perimeter, Volume	15		(4)	11		(3)	6		(4)	13		(3)	7		(3)	15		(3)		(20)	
R	Charts (Bar, Pie, Venn, Line)	16		(3)	9		(3)	7		(3)	15		(3)	5		(3)	16		(5)		(20)	
S	Ratio, Proportion, Factors, Multiples	17		(4)	8		(3)	8		(2)	16		(3)	n/a	X	(0)	19		(3)		(15)	
T	Time	18		(4)	7		(2)	9		(5)	17		(3)	4		(3)	17		(3)		(20)	
U	Money	9		(3)	6		(4)	10		(3)	18		(3)	3		(4)	18		(3)		(20)	
V	Length/Distance, Mass, Weight	3		(3)	20		(4)	12		(4)	19		(4)	n/a	X	(0)	n/a	X	(0)		(15)	
				(60)			(60)			(60)			(60)			(60)			(60)		(360)	

Printed in Great Britain
by Amazon

47617339R00059